Longman

GWERSLYF[...]

TEXTBOOK

W[...]

WRITI[...]

S R [...]

Longman

Titles in the series

Punctuation *Ian Gordon*

ABC of Common Errors *S H Burton*

Writing Letters *S H Burton*

Spelling *S H Burton*

Help Yourself to Study *Ralph Tabberer and Lesley Millard*

Grammar *S H Burton*

Improve Your Word Power *Sue Lloyd*

Get Yourself a Job *Roy Dyche*

LONGMAN GROUP UK LIMITED
Longman House
Burnt Mill, Harlow, Essex CM20 2JE, England
and Associated Companies throughout the world.

First published 1983
Ninth impression 1993
ISBN 0 582 25054 4

Set in 10/11pt Linotron Rockwell Light and Medium

Produced by Longman Singapore Publishers Pte Ltd
Printed in Singapore

The Publisher's policy is to use paper manufactured from
sustainable forests.

CONTENTS

INTRODUCTION

LONGMAN GROUP LIMITED
Longman House Burnt Mill Harlow Essex
CM20 2JE

25 August 1983

Dear Reader,

      Writing letters is a job that we all have to do from time to time, but many of us put it off until the last possible moment – and then, quite often, make a mess of it.

      The usual reason for this poor performance is lack of confidence. A lot of people aren't sure what is expected of them when they have to write a letter.

      You can't write a good letter unless you know the rules about form and lay-out. This short Guide deals with those first. They aren't complicated, so you can soon learn them.

      Then, it explains the differences between the various kinds of letters that have to be written. Different occasions require different treatment. The kind of letter that works in one situation won't be any good in others.

      The Guide also provides practice in writing the sorts of letters that you will need to tackle.

      Letter writing is an important task of daily life. I've tried to help you to do it well.

                  Yours sincerely,

                  S.H. Burton

THE RULES OF
LETTER WRITING

1 The letter writer's address

You want an answer to many of the letters you write, but you won't get an answer if you don't tell your reader your address!

Write your address in the top righthand corner of the sheet.

Make sure it is clear and pleasant to look at.

Choose the style of punctuation and lay-out that you prefer
>   *either* Style 1: closed punctuation/indented lines (see page 3)
>   *or* Style 2: open punctuation/blocked lines (see page 3)

REMEMBER   Both styles are correct. Neither is "better" than the other. Practise both. Choose the style that you can write clearly and neatly – the one that looks better.

Don't use lined paper. Plain paper is preferred. You must learn to keep your lines of writing level.

Style 1   *Closed punctuation/Indented lines*

> 52, Sharp Street,
> Millborough,
> Northshire.
> MB21 3CH

Notes

1 The county line (Northshire) ends with a full stop.
2 The earlier lines end with a comma.
3 The comma after the house number (52) is optional.
4 The postcode (MB21 3CH) is written as a separate line at the end of the address – *no* punctuation.
5 The lines of the address are "indented" – each line begins a little to the right of the line above.
6 The postcode line is *not* indented.

Style 2   *Open punctuation/Blocked lines*

> 52 Sharp Street
> Millborough
> Northshire
> MB21 3CH

Notes

1 There is no punctuation at all in the open punctuation style. That is why it is called *open* punctuation.
2 The lines are *not* indented. That is why they are called *blocked* lines.

NOTE   Both block and indent letters are shown in this book.

2 Addressing the envelope

You want your letter to reach its destination safely and without unnecessary delay, so address the envelope clearly and correctly.

Write the first line about halfway down the envelope. Keep this first line well clear of the stamp. The postmark(s) will blot out part of the address if you start too near the top.

Leave a margin at the lefthand side of the address, but write the address nearer to the lefthand edge of the envelope than the right.

Leave a space between the last line of the address (the postcode) and the bottom of the envelope.

Good positioning and spacing make for a well-addressed envelope.

Make sure your writing is clear. A badly-written envelope will cause delay in the post.

Choose *either* Style 1 *or* Style 2.

REMEMBER   The postcode is *always* the last line – *always* on its own – *never* punctuated – *never* indented.

Style 1   Closed punctuation/Indented lines

Mr J.F. Smith,
  36, High Street,
    Firthtown,
      Northumberland.
      NT13 10FT

Notes

   1 Mr is not followed by an abbreviation point.
   2 Check the other details of Style 1 in the Notes on
     page 3.

Style 2   Open punctuation/Blocked lines

Mr J F Smith
36 High Street
Firthtown
Northumberland
NT13 10FT

Notes

   1 *Open* punctuation – so *no* punctuation at all – not
     even after the recipient's initials (Mr J F Smith).
   2 Check the other details of Style 2 in the Notes on
     page 3.

3 Dating the letter

Letters should always be dated. The date on the letter is an important piece of information. Both the writer of the letter and its recipient may need to refer to it in later letters. For example:

Thank you for your letter of enquiry dated 21 July. If you will refer to our earlier letter of 3 July, acknowledging your order, you will see that we were unable to promise delivery of the short-wave radio (Model 262A) before the end of the month.

NOTE   Undated letters can be very confusing. How can you meet your aunt at the bus station "the day after tomorrow" when you don't know on what day the letter making that request was written?

Place the date beneath your address at the top of the sheet. That is the usual place for it in "private" correspondence. Letters typed in offices often have the date in a different place. (see pages 18 and 19)

Write the separate items of the date in this order

day   month   year

Date forms often used

21 January 1983	21 1 1983
21st January 1983	21 1 83
21st January, 1983	21. 1. 83
21 Jan., 83	21/1/83

Advice on choice of date form

1 Use a "clean" (uncluttered) date form.
2 You don't need st or th or rd after the day numeral.
3 You don't need a comma between the month and the year.
4 Abbreviations (e.g. Jan. and '83) are unsuitable for letters.
5 All-numeral date forms (e.g. 21/1/83) are suitable for invoices and other forms, but *unsuitable* for letters.

The recommended date form is 21 January 1983

REMEMBER
- *No* st after the day numeral
- *No* comma between the month and the year
- *No* abbreviations

NOTE   You will not be wrong if you use one of the other date forms, but the recommended form is clear, simple, "unfussy" – *and* it is widely accepted as the best way of writing the date on a letter.

4 *Dear So-and-so*

Having written your address and the date, you must next "greet" your reader.

This "greeting" (often called "the salutation") is the proper way of beginning. It is a signal that a message is being sent to the reader and it is a polite way of asking the reader to give that message his attention. The salutation is a courtesy that must never be left out.

The usual salutation is Dear so-and-so (Dear Mrs Smith or Dear Tom or Dear Mr Brown, etc.)

Place the salutation on the lefthand side of the sheet, lower down than your address and the date.

Leave a generous margin between the first word of the salutation and the lefthand edge of the sheet.

REMEMBER
- Dear (as the first word of the salutation) begins with a capital D.
- A comma at the end of the salutation is optional, but no other form of punctuation will do. *Never* end the salutation with a dash (–) or an oblique stroke (/). A comma or nothing.
- The salutation *always* stands as a line on its own.

12 Cross Lane,
Weltham,
Southshire.
SH 22 4WM
26 May 19 —

Dear Mrs Brown,
                    Thank you for sending
me such a lovely birthday present.

Notes

1 The salutation (Dear Mrs Brown) comes below the date and is written in the lefthand side of the sheet.

2 A margin is left between the beginning of the salutation and the lefthand edge of the sheet.

3 The salutation stands as a line on its own. The first line of the letter begins where the salutation ends. It is placed below the salutation and it begins with a capital letter (Thank you ...).

4 The comma at the end of the salutation is optional. The writer used a comma here because Style 1 (closed punctuation) was chosen for the address.

5 No abbreviation point after Mrs in the salutation.

5 Mr/Mrs/Miss – and so on

The "title of courtesy" or "style of address" before the name of the person you are writing to is an important part of the salutation – *Mr* Jones, *Miss* Smith, and so on.

The chief styles of address are

1 Dear John	1 Dear Jane
2 Dear Mr Jones	2 Dear Mrs/Miss/Ms Jones
3 Dear Sir	3 Dear Madam

REMEMBER

- The first-name-only style of address (Dear John/Dear Jane) is used when you are writing to friends of your own age, or to older people if they have asked you to use this "intimate" style.
- In most formal letters the Mr/Mrs/Miss/Ms style of address is used. (Other styles are used occasionally, see page 20.)
- After Mr and Mrs don't use an abbreviation point.
- Dear Sir and Dear Madam should be used *only* in very formal letters (often of a legal or business nature) between people who do not know each other personally.

6 Yours ...

Before signing a letter, the writer "rounds off" the message politely. This rounding off is called "the close". It must never be left out.

Informal letters may be rounded off with whatever close is suited to the relationship between the writer and the person being written to. For example: Yours ... Yours ever ... Yours affectionately ... Your loving niece ... and so on.

Formal letters **must** be rounded off with one of the usual endings.

The usual endings are

> Yours sincerely   Yours faithfully

Notes
1 Use Yours sincerely when you have greeted your reader (in the salutation) by his or her name – Dear Mr Jones/Dear Mrs Smith/Dear Ms Robinson.
2 *Never* use Yours sincerely when your opening is Dear Sir or Dear Madam.
3 Yours faithfully is the formal close. Use it when the salutation is equally formal – Dear Sir or Dear Madam.

REMEMBER

Salutation	*Close*
Dear Mr/Mrs/Miss/Ms Smith	Yours sincerely
Dear Sir or Dear Madam	Yours faithfully

7 Signing off

The close and the letter writer's signature (which comes below the close) are written at the bottom of the letter and in the righthand half of the sheet. Like this:

Dear Mr Jones,
> *the letter*

Yours sincerely,

Janice Smith

Notes
1 Capital Y (Yours). Small s (sincerely). NOTE spelling – sincerely.
2 The comma after Yours sincerely is optional. If you use a comma after Dear Mr Jones, use a comma after Yours sincerely. If you use a comma after Dear Sir/Dear Madam, use a comma after Yours faithfully.

REMEMBER Sign your letter properly

Salutation	*Close and signature*
1 Dear Charles,	Yours,
	Dick
2 Dear Mrs Brown,	Yours sincerely,
	Hilda White
3 Dear Madam,	Yours faithfully,
	Jean Thompson

Never include your title or style as part of your signature.

Mrs Alice Green   *Mr A. B. Robinson*

Do not put a full stop at the end of your signature.

8 The rules at work: a letter to study

56 Shrewsbury Avenue,
Fairpark,
Stafford.
ST32 17FP

15 July 19—

Dear Mrs Whyte,

Thank you for sending details of this summer's camp and for inviting me to join in. I was thinking only the other day that you'd soon have all the arrangements made, and I was wishing that I could be with you all.

I haven't joined the local Guides as yet. There hasn't been time since we moved. In any case, my friends are at Westfield and it will be much more fun to be in camp with them.

It is very good of you to say that I can stay at your house the night before camp begins. I couldn't get down to Westfield in time to leave with the rest of the party on their early morning start.

I'll find out about the coach services and let you know soon what time I'll be arriving on Friday 16 August.

My parents ask me to send you their best wishes.

Thank you again for being so kind.

Yours sincerely,
Brenda Brown

LETTERS OF DIFFERENT KINDS

1 What makes them different?

The differences are due to three things:
1 The *person* you are writing to   – the *recipient*
2 *What* you are writing about   – the *subject*
3 *Why* you are writing   – the *purpose*

A letter to a friend making holiday plans and a letter to a college asking for details of a course are two very different kinds of letters.

Why do the differences matter?

In the examples just mentioned, the opening in the letter to the friend is not suitable in the letter to the college. The endings must be different. The *whole way of writing* each letter must be different.

Letters can be grouped as being
    formal   *or*   informal

Formal letters can be either
    formal-impersonal   *or*   **formal-personal**

For example:
1 A letter to a tour operator asking for details of a package holiday is a formal-impersonal letter.
2 A letter to the mother of a friend of yours thanking her for a holiday is a formal-personal letter.
3 A letter to a friend of your own age congratulating him or her on an examination success will probably be written as an informal letter.

2 Examples of different kinds of letters

Formal-impersonal letters
Requests
- to firms, officials, organisations for information
- for help or co-operation from firms or public figures
- for permission from authorities

Letters
- of application for jobs or for membership of clubs
- answering invitations to attend for interview
- accepting/rejecting offers of employment
- ordering goods
- of enquiry about goods ordered
- of complaint
- making bookings or reservations
- confirming/cancelling bookings or reservations

Formal-personal letters
Letters
- of congratulation/condolence/apology/excuse
- to sick friends/relatives/acquaintances
- of (social) invitation
- replying to invitations
- saying "thank you" after holidays, outings, presents, favours, good turns

Personal letters
- written on a variety of occasions and subjects
- between friends of similar age and "standing"
- may express opinions or feelings
- may give or ask for information and personal news
- are free and easy in their use of letter-writing formalities and in the way they are written

REMEMBER the worst mistakes in letter writing are caused by mixing up the different kinds. For example: writing an informal letter when a formal one is needed; writing a formal-impersonal one instead of a formal-personal one.

IMPERSONAL LETTERS (FORMAL)

1 Sounding the right note

Formal-impersonal letters are written "to get things done". They are written about the "official" or "business" subjects of our lives, not the private and personal ones. When we write to a firm to order goods, we write as *customers*, not as "ourselves".

Formal-impersonal letters are written to firms and other organizations, to offices and departments, to employees of firms and to officials.

Because they are written to get things done, they are often called "business letters". Their other description – "formal-impersonal" – suggests the guidelines you should follow when you are writing this kind of letter.

1 *Formal* The rules of letter writing must be strictly obeyed. (For information about special "formalities" often found in business letters see pages 18 and 19.)

2 *Impersonal* These letters should be crisp and business-like. Write in a cool and level-headed way. Don't get excited. Concentrate on the *business* you are trying to get done. Don't bury it in irrelevant personal details. Always keep your eye on the job you are doing, and move along at a brisk pace.

Ask yourself – Why am I writing this letter? What *exactly* do I want it to do?

Plan your letter carefully

- How should I begin?
- What should come next?
- How do I end it?
- Is this a good, clear plan?
- Does each part of the letter follow on sensibly, or am I going round in circles?

Keep to the point. Don't include anything that does not strictly belong to the subject of the letter.

Be brief but don't leave out important details.

Be polite but don't waste words.

Write clear, simple English. The plainest way of putting things is the best.

Be careful with handwriting – sentences – paragraphs – punctuation – spelling. You are writing to get something done – something that matters to you. So don't give your reader the impression that you are careless.

The formal-impersonal letters on pages 23–31 show you how to do the job. (Some of them show you how *not* to do it!)

Formal

2 A formal-impersonal (business) letter

Study the letter on page 19. The notes on this page highlight special points of lay-out and style which you should use when writing a business letter.

1 The printed letter head supplies all the postal (and telephone) details needed for a reply. Write your own address neatly and accurately on every letter you write.

2 Our ref/Your ref enables office staff to file a copy of the letter – and to find it later! (BGG = the letter writer's initials/JJ = the letter typist's initials.) You can ignore these "Refs" *unless* you are asked to quote them (or another "Ref") in your reply.

3 The recipient's name and address always appear, either above the salutation (as here) or below the letter. It is both courteous and efficient to identify the recipient in this way. Do so when you reply.

4 The salutation and the close (Dear Sir ... Yours faithfully) are correct. This is a formal-impersonal, strictly business letter. Reply in the same style. After you become a member, Mr Good *may* change to Dear Mr Smith ... Yours sincerely. If he does, reply in the same way: Dear Mr Good ... Yours sincerely.

5 The letter is given a heading below the salutation. This acts as a sort of title, summing up the main subject of the letter. The heading helps the reader to "tune in" at once. Use the same heading in your reply.

6 Details (name and function in firm) after signature are helpful. You are told who is dealing with your business. Use those details in your reply – and on the envelope.

SLIPSTREAM MODELS LIMITED
63–69 Parnall Street   Westchester
Midshire   MD6 5WR
Telephone: (0366) 5762   Telex: 89251

Our ref BGG/JJ
Your ref

14 October 19-

Mr J K Smith
6 The Poplars
Harveston
Northumberland
NE11 12TP

Dear Sir

Slipstream Models Owners' Club : Membership
Application

Your letter of 10 October has been passed
to me and I now have pleasure in sending you
full details of Club Membership.

    If you will complete the enclosed
registration card and return it to me
with your remittance, you will at once
be enrolled as a member.

    Your Certificate of Membership, to-
gether with the current issue of Slipstream Club News, will be sent to you as
soon as I receive your official application.

    I am sure that Club Membership will
greatly increase your enjoyment of your
Slipstream Models and I look forward to
welcoming you to our Club.

Yours faithfully

B G Good

B G Good
Enrolling Secretary
Slipstream Models Owners' Club

Directors   T Mann (Managing)   Julia Green   F Jones
Registered office   14 Clive Street   London   WC3 14CS
Registered number   5652238   England

Formal

3 Notes on some special points

- *Mr or Esq?* Mr is the more common style of address, but Esq (short for Esquire) is still often used. Esq is preferred by some men, so you must be tactful and use it when you guess it is expected. The correct form is:

  J.H. Bloggins, Esq., (closed punctuation)

  J H Bloggins Esq   (open punctuation)

  Never use both Mr and Esq. It's one or the other – *not* both.

- *Dr   Professor   Reverend*

  Dr does not have an abbreviation point.

  Never shorten Professor to Prof.

  Reverend *in full* is best. Revd (no abbreviation point) is acceptable. Rev. is *not* recommended.

- *Ms* is the courteous and correct style for a woman when she does not indicate a preference for either Mrs or Miss.

- *Sir* is often used as the salutation when a letter (for publication) is written to the editor of a newspaper.

- *Dear Sirs* is the opening to use when you are writing to a firm.

- *Yours truly* was an acceptable alternative to *Yours faithfully*, but it's out of fashion.

- *I/We remain ...* This and other elaborate ways of ending are out of fashion.

REMEMBER   The modern fashion is for simplicity. If in doubt, go for the simple forms.

4 Plain style

The plainest way of putting things is the best. Letter writers often forget that advice. They try to impress their readers by using a long-winded pompous style of writing.
It doesn't work.

Avoid these faults
- **Popular and over-worked expressions**
  For example: "it is anticipated that" instead of "I expect ..."; "in this day and age" instead of "nowadays".

- **Would-be "important" words**
  For example: "purchase" instead of "buy"; "reside" instead of "live".

- **Roundabout expressions**
  For example: "in the region of" instead of "about"; "with all due expedition" instead of "as quickly as possible".

Try to be: simple   direct   brief

Ask yourself: **Have I put this in the shortest and clearest possible way?**

A model business letter

Dear Sir,
        I have repaired your bicycle. Please collect it as soon as you can.
                                Yours faithfully,
                                Joe Simmons

We can't always be as brief and direct as that – but we can try!

5 How to use the examples

The examples of letter writing on pages 23–31 are of three kinds:
1 Faulty letters for you to study and improve.
2 Good letters that you can use as guides.
3 Letters *on the same subject* printed on opposite pages so that you can compare them and see why one succeeds and the other fails.

6 Letter writing check list: a fault finder

Use this check list as a fault finder when you are working on the examples *and* when you are writing letters of your own.

- **The rules of letter writing** Has the writer used them properly? Are the "formalities" (e.g. salutation and close) suitable for this kind of letter?

- **Contents** Does the writer stick to the point? Are all *necessary* details included?

- **The way the letter is written** Too free-and-easy? Too stiff? Pompous? Clear? Simple? Direct? Brief? Long-winded? Too excitable? Sounds the right/wrong note?

- **Plan of Letter** Clear and logical? Does each part follow on sensibly, or is the writer going round in circles?

- **Paragraphs and sentences** Well made? Clumsy?

- **Punctuation and spelling** Accurate? Careless?

- **The master question** Is this letter likely to get the result that its writer wants?

Example A Request for permission to use a school hall

Study this letter, using the check list on page 22 as you go through it. Then write a letter on the same subject – one that you consider would be more likely to get the result that the writer wants.

13, Old Road, Fransham
Midshire MD6, 130R
17/6/19—

Dear Mr. Peters/ I'm writing about the South Street Primary School hall and want to know about using it on Saturday. It seems a pity it isn't used when the pupils aren't there. It would make a good rehearsal place for our dramatics.

Let me know soon,

Yours Faithfully
Mr. J. Brown.

P.S I'm the secretary of the Fransham Amateur Players. Write to me at my home address which is same as written above.

P.P.S Being Director of Education I was told you're the person to ask. We're putting on our next play soon, so this is urgent.

Thank you.

Example B   A business letter and a reply

Study the letter on this page and Janet Jones's reply on page 25. Each letter is correct, clearly expressed and well suited to do the job its writer intends it to do.

page 25

UNIVERSAL POSTAL BARGAINS LTD
110 Thrift Street
Milltown   MT16 12HS
Tel. 03322-57686

Our ref PMT/sb

Your ref

15 July 19-

Mrs J Jones
5 The Crescent
Greendale
Lancashire
GR11 5LS

Dear Madam

Shirtblouse Style 3A Colour MB Size 12

Thank you for your letter of 10 July and postal order (No.HP276210) for the sum of £5.95.

Unfortunately, our stocks of this garment in polyester/cotton were exhausted within a few days of our advertisement in the national press.

However, we have ample stocks in the style, colour and size that you ordered, but in nylon, and we shall be pleased to send one of these if it meets with your requirements.

Should you decide not to accept this substitution, we shall, of course, refund your money at once.

Perhaps you will be good enough to let us have your instructions.

Yours faithfully,

P M Thorn

P M Thorn
Manager
Mail Order Department

Directors C S Robinson (Managing)   Henrietta Tonks
Registered office   as above
Registration number   353762   England

---

5 The Crescent,
Greendale,
Lancashire.
GR11 5LS

17 July 19

The Manager,
Mail order Department,
Universal Postal Bargains Ltd.

Dear Sir,

<u>Shirt blouse Style 3A Colour MB Size 12</u>

Thank you for your letter of 15 July.
I am sorry to learn that you have sold
out of the polyester / cotton shirt blouses.
I do not want this garment in nylon,
so I shall be obliged if you will refund
my money as soon as possible.

yours faithfully,
Janet Jones

JANET JONES

Example C Letter reserving accommodation

This letter has some good points, but it is *not* likely to get the result that its writer wanted. Apply the check list on page 22. Note especially points 2, 3 and 4. Then see what improvements you can make.

---

65 Cresswell Street,
Tollgate,
Northshire.
NS36 4CW

3 May 19–

The Manager,
The Railway Hotel,
East Sands,
Southshire.
SH11 9RH

Dear Sir,

    Your attractive advertisement in our local paper, the "Tollgate Times", was very interesting, and so I am writing to book a week's holiday with my sister in August.

    We shall want you to meet us with the hotel car at Sandstone station. You said that you could arrange this at no extra cost.

    We want a twin-bed room with a view of the sea and I'd better order full board, including lunches. Please note that we shan't always be in for lunch, though. We are both very fond of walking and we shall be out when the weather is fine. We have decided on a holiday at East Sands because of its well-known cliff walks.

    I look forward to an early reply and to your confirmation of this booking.

Yours faithfully,
Arabella Stuart

Example D Letter of complaint

Is this a good letter? What job did its writer intend it to do? Will it do that job? Check it with the fault finder on page 22.

Check it with the fault finder on page 22.

---

7 The Glebe
Pontchester
Midshire
MD9 3TG

25 January 19–

Formal

The Managing Director
Newstyle Products Ltd
Bostock
West Heartlands
WH1 1NH

Sir

For Christmas my grandfather gave me one of your cameras – expensive at that – not from your cheap range – and I think you ought to know that it's already cost me a lot in wasted films. The trouble is there wasn't an instruction book with it and the shop it was bought from can't (or won't) get one. I can't afford to go on feeding it with expensive films and not getting good pictures. They're terrible. It's one of those that you make with automatic exposure, but the shop can't tell me how to work it.

You must agree, it's a disgrace and I want to know what you are going to do about it.

Write by return to:

Mr Peter J Snapper

Example E   Requesting help from a firm   (two letters)

This letter is not at all good. The writer has not given enough thought to its contents. Important details are missing and irrelevant ones are included. It is not clear. The language is often unsuitable. Worst of all, it sounds quite the wrong note. The writer has forgotten that he is asking a favour. He thinks that he is demanding a right.

17 Charles Road,
Midhampton,
Toneshire.
TS22 7CR

10 March 19–

Print and Dyestuffs Ltd.,
23 New Estate,
Midhampton,
Toneshire.
TS11 8NE

Dear Sirs,
            Starting in April, I'm working on a project and I'd like your help. I need all the information I can get about industry in this area. I've got to produce a report of several hundred words by the end of June, so I want to get cracking as soon as I've had an Easter break.
            It will be convenient if you send me your usual information pack by the end of this month at the latest.
            Thanking you for your cooperation, I am,
                        Yours, etc.

Horace T Walpole

Horace T Walpole

Compare this letter with the one on page 28.

5A The Wentworths
Midhampton
Toneshire
TS5 7TW

10 March 19–

The Company Secretary
Print & Dyestuffs Ltd
23 New Estate
Midhampton
Toneshire
TS11 8NE

Dear Sir

Project: a survey of new industry in the Midhampton district

     I am working on this project and I need information about firms that have recently moved into the area. Your firm is one of the largest of these, so I shall be very grateful if you can spare the time to help me.

     Three points are specially important:

1 Training schemes for school leavers;
2 Transport arrangements to overcome poor road and rail links in this district;
3 Plans for expansion.

     Any other information will be useful, but those points are the ones with which I most need your help.

     I apologise for adding to your work with this request, but I do hope that you will feel able to assist me.

Yours faithfully

Kate Spencer

Kate Spencer

Encl. Stamped, addressed envelope

Formal

Example F Enquiry (two letters)

Compare this letter with the improved version on the page opposite.

Use the check list on page 22 to help you to make a detailed comparison of the two.

62, High Street
Crofton.

Dear Sir/

Can you help me, I hope so. I'm looking for a record that isn't in our local shop and they told me that it's one of yours. It's one that Trouble and Strife have made and I heard it one morning on the radio when (as usual!) I was dashing to get ready to catch my bus so I didn't hear any details.

It must be around if Record Spin had it, because they don't play old ones. You'll know about Record Spin, I expect.

If you send it, I'll send the money. I want it soon for a present. It's my brother's birthday next week and he's mad on Trouble and Strife, though they aren't my favourites.

Thanks.

Miss S. Player

Miss S. Player

P.S. It was good, so I expect you'll know which one I mean. I know they make a lot, but it's just this one I want. Thanks again.

Although this is a much better letter than the one opposite, you may think that it could be improved in some ways. Make any changes that you can think of to tighten it up and to make it crisper, but don't bully the firm!

62 High Street,
Crofton,
Surrey.
CT6 21HT

30 May 19–

Trumpet Records Limited
Music House
6–8 Caverswall Avenue
London
SE4 1CA

Dear Sirs,

On Tuesday 27 May a single by Trouble and Strife was played towards the end of Record Spin (BBC Radio 1). I'd like to buy a copy, but I was in a hurry to leave the house and I missed the details of title, number, etc.

I have been told that all recent recordings by this Group have been issued under your label, but our local shop (Discreet – Broad Street – Crofton) cannot trace the record I want.

Please send me your catalogue. I think I shall recognize the title when I see it. Then, I can order the record through Discreet.

I think that you ought to see that Discreet has a copy of your catalogue, and they ought to stock your records. It's not very convenient to have to write.

Yours faithfully,

Sara Player

Sara Player

JOB APPLICATIONS – FORMS AND LETTERS

1 What the employer wants

Applicants are usually asked to complete an application form *or* to write a letter of application *or* to do both.

Whichever is asked for, the information you must give falls into these groups:

1 **Personal details** Age; state of health; schools attended; present circumstances.

2 **Qualifications** Exam results; any certificates or awards.

3 **Experience** Previous/present job(s); part-time job(s); any other experience (particular interests, work for voluntary groups, and so on) bearing on the job you are applying for.

4 **Any other details** that seem to fit the candidate for the job.

That information *and the way it is presented* are what the employer uses to decide which candidates to interview.

If you fill in the form properly and write a good letter, you may get an interview. If you don't – you won't!

2 What you must do

You'll find detailed advice on pages 33–41. First, here are three rules that you must obey.

1 Be neat, clear and accurate. An untidy careless applicant won't get an interview.
2 Be truthful and don't exaggerate.
3 Try to highlight your strong points – those that make **you** suitable for **this** job.

3 Application form

1 Read it right through before you begin to answer it. You'll avoid overlaps and repetitions. Also, a later question may throw light on how to answer an earlier one.
2 Draft your answers on spare paper. The place for mistakes and corrections is the spare paper *not* the form.
3 Use black or dark blue ink. The completed form may be photocopied and this photocopies well.
4 Keep a copy of the questions and your answers. You may need to refer to them at interview – or when making other applications.
5 Give the information you are asked for, not what you think you ought to have been asked for.
6 Don't draw attention to your weak points. Unless you are told to answer every question, blanks are better than a form peppered with "No" – "None" – "No experience" – etc.
7 Try to give positive answers. For example, it's better to write "I am looking for a new opportunity" than to write "My present job is a dead end".
8 If there is an "Any Other Information" space, use it. But don't repeat information already given. Draw attention to personal qualities/experience that fit *you* for *this* job. Don't try to cram everything in. Write one or two clear sentences about your special fitness to do this job – not a ragbag of afterthoughts.

4 *Covering letter*

Instructions to job applicants often go like this: "The completed form, together with a covering letter in the applicant's own handwriting, should be returned to – (name of employer) by – (last date for accepting applications)."

The covering letter is sometimes referred to as "a letter in support of your application" – and that is what you must try to write. It gives you an opportunity to strengthen your chances, but only if you

REMEMBER these rules:

1. *Don't* simply repeat information already given on the application form. A candidate for a job who does that is wasting his own and the employer's time.
2. *Don't* ramble. The covering letter must be carefully planned – a tight piece of writing – everything to the point.
3. *Do* highlight the strongest point(s) in your favour. Draw attention to personal qualifications and/or experience that specially fit you for this job *and say (briefly, clearly and firmly) why you believe that you are right for the job.*

This covering letter shows you how it should be done. (Addresses have been left out here to save space.)

Dear Madam,

    Junior receptionist: Foxbridge Health Centre

      I am enclosing my application form for this post. I believe that my answers to the questions show that I am a suitable applicant.

      My experience as a part-time volunteer at the St John's Ambulance Brigade Headquarters in Foxbridge (see section 4 of the form) is my strongest qualification.

      The training I had as a switchboard operator would be useful to me in a busy health centre. I also worked in the records office. Most important is the fact that I had experience (under supervision) as a receptionist, helping the members of the public who called at the headquarters office with enquiries.

      My St John's Superintendent (the first of the referees named on the form) was pleased with my work.

      I enjoyed the experience and it has made me keen to find full-time employment in similar work. I am sure that, with the training you give, I could soon become a useful member of your staff.

            Yours faithfully,

            Ann Smith

            ANN SMITH

5 Letter of application

When only a letter of application is asked for (no form), your letter has to do all the work. It must give all the necessary information and highlight your strong points.

REMEMBER
- to be careful with the *presentation* – the way your letter *looks* and the correct use of the "formalities" of letter writing;
- to *plan* its contents – think out very carefully what you are going to write and the best order in which you can make your, points. (see pages 40 and 41)

Make a draft on spare paper. You can't expect to get the letter right first time. Crossings-out and alterations belong to your draft, not to the letter you send off.

The rules of letter writing must be strictly obeyed. You won't get an interview if your letter indicates that you don't know how to set a letter out correctly.

Handwriting and presentation must be good – your best and clearest handwriting.

Punctuation and spelling must be accurate. Carelessness will put an employer off. Use a dictionary. Get somebody to "vet" your letter for you before you send it off.

Give your letter a heading A letter of application must be crisp – clear – business-like. A suitable heading helps you to write a letter with those good qualities. Place the heading below the salutation and above the first line of your letter. Underline it – use a ruler!

References You are often asked to include references in your letter of application. The instructions are usually worded like this: "references must be provided" *or* "write … with references" *or* "supply the names and addresses of (number) referees".

"References" means the names and addresses of people who are willing to write about you (in confidence) to the employer. The people who write such letters are called "referees".

Sometimes, the number of references required is stated. If the number is not stated, try to supply three. Even if references are not asked for, always give the name and address of at least one responsible person who is willing to give the employer his confidential opinion of you and of your suitability for the job.

REMEMBER *Always* ask your referees for permission to use their names. Tell them what job(s) you are applying for and what you think your strong points are.

Jobs

Here are three typical job advertisements. (To save space they are printed in complete lines, not "displayed" as they were in the newspapers.) All three ask for a letter only and indicate that the letter must be handwritten.

- **Job 1** Jones Bros. Ltd. Tools and Home Supplies. Require one young sales person. Apply in own handwriting to the Manager, Jones Bros. Ltd., 32 Hansom Row, Powderton, PD3 12HR.

- **Job 2** Junior Assistant required in small but busy Accounts Office. Must be intelligent, of neat and pleasant appearance, in good health. Mathematically competent. Able to work on own initiative. Apply in writing to Box No. 507, Weekly Record, 6 Mill Lane, Cheesebury, CB11 6ML.

- **Job 3** Shop assistant required. Apply in writing only, stating full details of qualifications and experience, and including references. Fashions Unlimited, 11 High Street, Withyford, WY2 4HS.

Notes

1 Only one advertiser states that references are required. Remember the advice given on page 37 and supply at least one reference for each job. Job 2, for example, (Accounts Office) is certainly the kind of job for which applicants would be expected to supply references. Job 3 asks for references but doesn't state how many. Try to give three.

2 Try to "read between the lines" as you study the job description. For example, the first advertisement doesn't seem to tell you a lot about the job, but if you use your wits you'll spot some useful clues. *Tools and Home Supplies* suggests that evidence of interest and some skill in carpentry,

craft work of any kind, motor vehicles, or household repairs ("D.I.Y." jobs) might get you an interview. Check, if you can, by a visit to the shop. This is the sort of "detective work" that is needed.

3 Try to "follow the leads" as you study the advertisement. For example, Job 2 – "Able to work on own initiative". Follow that up if you can – experience with clubs, societies (in and out of school), responsibilities successfully carried out, projects and activities led.

Special points

Job 1 Address envelope to: The Manager, Jones Bros. Ltd. ... etc. Use the same wording for the recipient's address on the first sheet of your letter. *Salutation* Dear Sir. *Close* Yours faithfully.

Job 2 Address envelope to: Box No. 507 ... etc. Use the same wording for the recipient's address on the letter. *Salutation* Dear Sirs. *Close* Yours faithfully.

Job 3 Address envelope to: Fashions Unlimited ... etc. Use the same wording for the recipient's address on the letter. *Salutation* Dear Sirs. *Close* Yours faithfully.

Jobs

Use this plan

1 *Personal details* Age, state of health, present situation (at school? – when leaving? – left? – now doing what?). The job description will show what else (if anything) should be added here. For example, Job 2: "... neat and pleasant appearance ...". Send a photograph with your application. Refer here to fact that you are doing so.

2 *Qualifications* List all exam results (*with dates*). Include any other qualifications (obtained in or out of school). *Proof* of achievement in, for example, music, sport, can be important.

3 *Experience* List any jobs done (*with dates*). Part-time work (paid or not) should be included. Study job description for clues.

4 *Any other details* that prove *your* suitability for *this* job. This is where you *highlight* your strong points. Don't be afraid of claiming *quietly* but *firmly* that you are the sort of applicant the employer is looking for. Study the letter on page 35 – Ann Smith did it well.

5 *End* with a brief statement of your interest in the job and your attitude to it. See end of Ann Smith's letter. Without overdoing it, she "came through" as a *person* with a *positive* approach.

Letter of application – the complete plan

1   your address

2   date

3   recipient's name and address

4   salutation

5   heading for letter

6   the letter itself
     i   personal details
    ii   qualifications
   iii   experience
   iv   any other details – highlighting your strong
        points
    v   brief statement of your personal and posi-
        tive approach to job

7   close

8   signature

9   name printed below signature

10 references
     "Reference may be made to the following:"
       names and addresses

     or

     "The following have agreed to act as my
     referees:"
       names and addresses

Jobs

6 Formal-impersonal letters for practice

Study the situations outlined, then write a letter suited to each.

1 You are the secretary of a youth organization (music/dramatic society, sports club, etc.). Your committee has asked you to write to the officer of your local authority to book a public hall in which you want to hold an event. You don't know what the booking fee is. Your club hasn't got much money. Perhaps there may be a reduction – even free booking – for a club such as yours?

2 A month ago, you ordered goods (enclosing payment) from Snugclothes, Railway Yard, Brithinshawe, BH7 4RH. You haven't received the goods and you haven't had an acknowledgement of your order. In the meantime, you have seen similar goods in a local shop at a lower price. You want to cancel your order, get your money back, and buy the cheaper goods.

3 Reply to this advertisement. Goldilocks, 15–17 High Street, Millchester, Midshire, MS11 4HS requires a junior improver to start in September. Excellent prospects for intelligent, hard-working youngster. Pleasing appearance and fashion sense are looked for. Full training given. Apply in writing by (date), with references.

4 You have lost a CSE (or other exam) certificate. Write to the secretary of your exam board asking whether you can be supplied with a replacement.

5 You decide to use your own initiative in job hunting. Write to the personnel officer of a local firm enquiring about the prospects of the kind of employment for which you are suited.

PERSONAL LETTERS (FORMAL)

1 Sounding the right note

"The worst mistakes in letter writing are caused by mixing up the different kinds ...". Make sure that you don't write an impersonal letter when you ought to write a personal one.

Why? Because the *wrong kind* of letter *can't* sound the *right* note – and your reader won't like it.

REMEMBER   Formal-personal letters are different from formal-impersonal letters because *the relationship between the writer and the reader is different and the letters are written about different kinds of things.*

Formal-impersonal (business)
1 letter writer *does not* know reader personally
2 purpose of letter is *to get something done* – writer and reader think of each other in an "official", "public", or "business" way – e.g. local government officer/member of public – job applicant/employer – customer/trader

Formal-personal
1 letter writer *does* know reader personally
2 purpose of letter is to send a message from one *person* to another *person* – subject of letter is some shared interest(s) in people, things, events

Personal

2 What you must do

Formal-personal letters are *formal* – so, remember:

1 Don't be slapdash. Your reader won't think much of you if your letter isn't properly set out and carefully written.
2 The salutation names the recipient: Dear Mr/Mrs/Miss/Ms Brown or Dear John/Jane.
3 The close is Yours sincerely.
4 *Never* use Dear Sir/Madam ... Yours faithfully.

Formal-personal letters are *personal* – so, remember:

1 You are writing as one *person* to another *person*.
2 You are *not* writing about a "business" or an "official" subject.
3 The *way* you write the letter must show your reader that you are thinking of him/her in a personal way.

3 How not to do it

> Dear Mrs Brown,
>
>   Thank you for the birthday present which arrived yesterday. I have many letters to write, so please accept this brief acknowledgement of your kind thought.
>
>   Yours sincerely,
>   Tom Robinson

Tom Robinson didn't mean to be rude – but he was! He wrote the wrong kind of letter, and he probably made Mrs Brown feel hurt and angry.

4 You and your reader

You are writing to a *person*. You must choose your words to suit:

1 the kind of relationship you have with that person
2 the kind of subject you are writing about

You wouldn't write to the mother of a friend thanking her for a present in the same way that you would write to the secretary of your sports club putting forward your ideas for changes in the programme. Yet both are formal-personal letters.

Here are some things to bear in mind

- much older/older   – about same age
- position of authority – equal "standing"
- not known long   – known a long time
- acquaintance   – (close) friend
- not related   – related
- not a lot in common   – many things in common

If you think about those things before you start to write a formal-personal letter, you will get yourself on the right lines.

Personal

5 Think it out

Before you begin, think about *why* you are going to write the letter. Thinking about *why* will suggest ideas about *what* to write and *how* to write it.

EXAMPLE Suppose you are going to write a letter to somebody who is ill:

Why am I going to write? Because I know him/her and I'm sorry he/she is ill. Because people who are ill like to know that other people are sorry and want them to get well. Because people who are ill often feel cut off and depressed. Hearing news about things and people that interest them cheers them up. I think that he/she will like to hear about ...

Thinking about why you are going to write has suggested plenty of ideas for your letter. A plan has taken shape:

1 Sorry to hear about your illness – hope you'll soon be better.
2 Saw X Y Z the other day. They asked me to send you their good wishes.
3 Thought you'd like to hear what happened at ....
4 Miss you at .... Looking forward to seeing you there soon.
5 Thinking about you and wishing you well.

Whenever you have a letter to write – whatever the subject – think it out like that before you start to write.

Example A   Thank-you letter

We all have to write thank-you letters. Too many
people just "go through the motions". They write a
colourless, "polite" letter. You should try to give
your reader pleasure by making him/her feel that
you really did enjoy the present/outing/holiday –
whatever it was for which you are saying thank you.
Here is a good example of how to do it.

7, Steep Street,
Willowtown,
Hampshire.
HH14 7ST

3 July 19＿

Dear Mrs Jones,

    Thank you very much for taking
me with you on that splendid outing to London.
It was the first time that I had seen the Tower
or any of the other famous sights. If I'd gone
alone, I couldn't have seen nearly as much,
because I wouldn't have known my way about.

    I think the river trip was the best
thing of all. London really came alive for me as
we saw it from the Thames during that wonderful
journey down to Greenwich.

    It was all tremendously exciting –
a day that I shall never forget.

    Thank you for giving me such a
great birthday treat.

                Yours sincerely,
                Betty.

Personal

Example B Sympathy (two letters)

Compare the letter on this page with the one on the opposite page. Which do you think is the better of the two? Make a list of the faults in the poor letter. (Turn back to pages 22 and 46 if you need help.)

15 Haughton Road

Dear Sir,

I saw Pete Green the other day and he told me you're in hospital and likely to be there for a good long time.

It's bad news for me because I was hoping you'd be coaching us in April. I think I've a pretty good chance of getting into the first team this summer and your coaching would have been a help to me. I suppose I must do my best without you.

Anyway, it's bad luck for us both that you've cracked up but perhaps you won't be in dock for as long as Pete thought.

yours
E Johnson

31 Waterloo Street,
Littlemoor,
Wiltshire.
WS20 2LM
31 March 19 —

Dear Mr Jenkins,

I saw Pete Green at the club yesterday and he told me about your sudden illness. I am very sorry and I do hope that you will soon be fit again.

If you are not able to run your cricket classes in April it will be a great loss to us all. Your coaching has made all the difference to us. I know that I, for one, would never have got into the first eleven without your help.

I'd like you to know that all the club members I saw yesterday were talking about you and wishing you well. I'm sure you'll be hearing from them.

We all hope to see you at the club again before long, in good health and — when summer comes — hitting many a six.

Yours sincerely,

James Smith

Personal

Example C Congratulations (two letters)

One of these letters is much better than the other. Both are correct in their use of the letter writing rules, but one of the writers has gone wrong with the writer-reader relationship. Nor has she thought about *why*, *what* and *how*.

16B Flower Lane,
Roundwell,
Essex.
ES30 5RW

15 June 19—

Dear Miss Chalk,

The news was in last week's local rag, and my mum said I ought to write to you. I expect you're over the moon about it.

You've done well, mum says, to be made head teacher at the Roundwell Middle School and she says you'll be missed at the Primary, where you've been teaching for so long.

It seems a long time since you taught me there. Of course, it is – I'm sixteen now, as you know. Still, we've kept up, with you being a neighbour and seeing mum at a lot of local get-togethers.

It'll be a big change but I hope you'll settle in all right. No time for more.

Yours sincerely,
Penny

18 Rose Walk
Roundwell
Essex
ES30 1BDW

15 June 19-

Dear Miss Chalk

Congratulations on your appointment as
headteacher at Roundwell Middle School. I read
the good news in last week's "Echo".

It was nice to read what was written about your
time at Roundwell Primary. I think the reporter
must have been talking to some of your old pupils
to be able to write what he did.

I'm sure that we all remember what you did
for us. I know I do. I've often been grateful to th
when I was at school and afterwards in my job.

It's good to know that you won't be moving
away and that you'll be able to carry on with
your local activities.

They are lucky to have you at the Middle
School, and I'm sure you'll be as happy and
successful there as you have been at the Primary
School.

Best wishes.

yours sincerely

Jenny Walker

Example D Invitation

When you write a letter of invitation, be specially careful about these three things:

1 *Details of date, place, time, and so on* Give all the necessary information and don't leave room for misunderstandings. You don't want a guest to arrive on the wrong day – or too early – or when the party is half over. Be tactful when you explain these details. You musn't sound as if you are giving orders to the person you're inviting.

2 *The personal touch* Make your invited guest feel that he/she really will be welcome. You *do* want him/her to accept. Don't overdo it, of course, but don't sound cold and unwelcoming.

3 *The writer-reader relationship* You must "tune in" to the relationship and make sure that what you write fits it. This is especially important when you are writing to someone older or someone who is not a close friend. Getting the writer-reader relationship right is always important, but particularly when you are writing a "social" letter of this kind.

Most of the problems that you find when you are writing any formal-personal letter are present in letters of invitation. Study the example on page 53. Jack Jones wrote a good letter because he "tuned in" to the writer-reader relationship and he thought out the *why*, the *what* and the *how*.

8 Leigh Road,
Bramcaster,
West Yorkshire.
WY12 8LR
30 September 19–

Dear Mr Field,

Thank you for your letter of congratulation on my exam results. I was very pleased to hear from you. The results were a great relief. I did much better than I thought I would.

We are having a celebration party on Saturday 15 October and we shall be pleased if you can come. It's a party for me, but my parents and some of their old friends are joining in, so you will find 'real people' as well as teenagers to talk to!

The party starts at half-past six – drinks; and a buffet supper later. You said in your letter that you've given up driving, so my father will meet you with the car at Bramcaster station. Please let me know what time your train arrives.

There's a good train back to Jessingham at 11.15 and we'll arrange transport for you to catch that. I hope that won't be too late for you. It would be a pity if you had to leave while the party was still in full swing.

I do hope that you will be able to come.

Yours sincerely,
Jack Jones

Personal

Example E Letter to a public person

You may have the job of writing to a well-known person asking him/her for help. For example: to give a talk to a club or society (sport, music, etc.) – open a fete, or a new scout/guide hut, or youth club, and so on.

1 Although you may not know the celebrity personally, your letter should be formal-*personal*. You know him/her by reputation. His/her distinction (in sport, show-business, community life, etc.) has made him/her known to everybody. So, the salutation *names* him/her: Dear Mrs .../Dear Professor .../Dear Dr .../Dear Jimmy Striker/Dear Jenny Nightingale (if that is how he/she is known to the public). The close is Yours sincerely.

2 Writer-reader relationship is very important. He/she is famous and busy. You are writing as an admirer asking a favour.

3 *Why*, *what*, and *how* must be thought out. You must try to be crisp and clear without being stiff. Your letter has to get something done, yet sound a personal note.

4 Plan your letter along these lines: identify yourself – reason for writing – exactly what you want him/her to do – date, time, place, length of talk/ceremony – how large and what sort of an audience – why his/her help matters – gratitude and appreciation of all concerned.

5 Enclose a stamped addressed envelope for his/her reply.

Here is a good example of a letter to a well-known person, asking a favour. Use it as a guide if you have to write a letter of this kind.

8 Saltash Street,
Miltonville,
Lincolnshire.
LS15 6MV

12 August 19–

Dear Tommy Adams,

As secretary of the Milton-
ville Under-Eighteen Sports Club, I am arranging
our winter programme.

We hold training sessions
and discussions on Tuesday and Thursday even-
ings, and the committee is inviting well-known
sports personalities to come to some of these. We
shall be pleased and honoured if you will be our
guest speaker at one of our meetings.

Please let me know which of
the following dates would be suitable for you:
Tuesday 14 October; Thursday 13 November;
Tuesday 9 December.

We meet at 7.30 p.m. in the
sports hall at the Miltonville Upper School in
Gladram Street and our meetings end at 9 p.m.

We'd like you to speak for
about half an hour and then be kind enough to
answer questions. We hope that you will talk
about your recent victory in the Regional Tennis
Championship and, of course, any advice you can
give us on improving our standards will be most
valuable.

I know you are busy and this
is asking a lot, but we have some keen tennis
players who will benefit from your help.

Yours sincerely,

Marjorie King

Marjorie King

6 Formal-personal letters for practice

1 An old friend of your family has invited you to stay. Before you reply, a friend of your own age suggests that the two of you should go for a holiday at that time. Your father/mother says, "Do as you like, but you must write a nice letter to Mr/ Mrs –. It was kind of him/her to invite you and you musn't hurt his/her feelings." Write a suitable letter of excuse.

2 You read in your local paper that a friend of yours has achieved a considerable success in some activity (music, sport, dramatics, etc.). While you were at school together, your friendship was close and you took part in this activity together. Your friend and his/her family then moved away from the district and you haven't seen each other or been in touch for some time. Write a suitable letter of congratulation.

3 Your father's/mother's oldest friend has been elected to your local council. Though you are not a bit interested in local politics yourself, you are told that it will please him/her if you write a letter of congratulation. Reluctantly, you agree. Go ahead!

4 On your birthday, you receive a present from a relative. Its arrival makes you realise that you forgot to send him/her a birthday card. You have never forgotten his/her birthday before and you cannot understand why you did so this time. Write a suitable letter of thanks and apology.

5 You have been camping with friends on a site owned by a friend of your father. He writes to you saying that damage was done to his fences. You know nothing about this and you feel sure that your companions were not responsible. Write a suitable letter.

INFORMAL LETTERS

The free-and-easy nature of informal letters has been pointed out (page 15), but this doesn't mean that they should be written in a slapdash way.

REMEMBER

1 "Identify" yourself. It's annoying to get a letter from someone who assumes that you know his/her address, when you don't. In any case, the writer should save the recipient the trouble of searching for it.

2 Always date the letter.

3 Writer-reader relationship is just as important in these as in other kinds of letters. These are the most *personal* letters of all, so you must write with your reader's personality and interests very much in mind. You will get the response you want *only* if you write a letter that is "tuned in" to the person who is going to read it – a letter that *suits the relationship that you have with that person.*

4 You must put a lot of yourself into an informal letter. You must show your understanding of the feelings and interests of your reader. You must try to make intelligent guesses about how your reader will respond to the way you are writing.

5 To sum up, a good informal letter is:

personal   lively   "beamed at" its
reader.

Informal

REMINDERS

1 Method

1 Before you start to write, ask yourself
   A *Who* is going to read this letter?
   B *Why* am I going to write this letter?
2 Thinking about *who* and *why* helps you to sort out
   A *what* you are going to write
   B *how* you are going to write it
3 To sum up, don't start to write until you have thought hard about
   A your reader
   B your subject
   C your aim
   D your plan
   E your style (*how* to write – your choice of words)
4 Write a draft of your letter on spare paper
5 Read the draft. As you read, "switch round" – see it through your reader's eyes.
6 Make the improvements that 5 suggests
7 Write your letter

2 Style

1 The plainest way of expressing yourself is the best.
2 "Contractions" (e.g. *I'd* = I should or I would/ *we'll* = we shall or we will/*shouldn't* = should not) are *not* suitable for formal-impersonal letters.
3 Slang is *not* suitable for any formal letter. And don't overdo it when you write informal letters. Why? Because it is an over-worked, stale, way of writing. Using slang makes you seem lazy – as if you can't be bothered to find your own way of expressing yourself.
4 When you are writing about a commercial trans-action (you are going to pay for something), be polite, but don't overdo it. For example, write "Please send ..." *not* "I shall be most grateful if you will send ...".
5 When you are asking a favour, then show your appreciation – "very grateful"/"I am sorry to trouble you"/"it will be a great help if ...". You are asking your reader to go to some trouble on your behalf, so let him/her know that you are aware of that fact.

3 Presentation

1 Obey the rules of letter writing – always.
2 Write in your best handwriting. If you are "a bad writer", do something about it. Take trouble – practise – and you will improve. Clarity and neatness always matter.
3 Take trouble over lay-out. Good spacing of lines and attractive positioning of the various parts of the letter (addresses, salutation, close, etc.) make all the difference to its look and, therefore, to the impression that it makes on its reader.
4 Be careful with spelling and punctuation. You must get them right.

Reminders